**BRIGHT
IDEA
BOOKS**

HOW DO
Sloths
POO?

Nancy Furstinger

raintree

a Capstone company — publishers for children

Raintree is an imprint of Capstone Global Library Limited, a company incorporated in England and Wales having its registered office at 264 Banbury Road, Oxford, OX2 7DY – Registered company number: 6695582

www.raintree.co.uk
myorders@raintree.co.uk

Edited by Maddie Spalding
Designed by Becky Daum
Production by Melissa Martin
Printed and bound in India

ISBN 978 1 4747 7513 7
22 21 20 19 18
10 9 8 7 6 5 4 3 2 1

British Library Cataloguing in Publication Data
A full catalogue record for this book is available from the British Library.

Acknowledgements
iStockphoto: andyjkramer, 9, dene398, 19, fotopitu, 22–23, Freder, 14–15, GeorgePeters, 25, 31; Newscom: Michael & Patricia Fogden/Minden Pictures, 26; Science Source: Kevin Schafer, 5; Shutterstock Images: Damsea, 10–11, cover (sloth), emka74, cover (poop), JohannesOehl, 20, kungverylucky, 13, Pavel Hlystov, 6–7, Sharp, 16–17, 28
Design Elements: iStockphoto, Red Line Editorial, and Shutterstock Images

We would like to thank Andy Grass, PhD, Assistant Professor of Anatomy at the New York Institute of Technology College of Osteopathic Medicine for his invaluable help in the preparation of this book.

CONTENTS

CHAPTER 1

POO Dance

A sloth climbs down a tree. The sloth reaches the ground. It clings to the tree. This helps it stay upright. Then it does a poo dance. The sloth wiggles its bottom.

Its tail digs a hole. The sloth squats. Small balls of poo come out. The poo plops into the hole. The sloth also wees into the hole. The sloth kicks dirt over its poo and wee.

Sloths usually poo on the ground.

Sloths sleep for about ten hours each day.

The sloth climbs back up the tree. The sloth is tired. It has used up a lot of energy! It settles in for a nap.

WEAK MUSCLES

A sloth's leg muscles are weak. Sloths often hold onto trees when they poo. This helps them to stay steady.

CHAPTER 2

SLOW AND Sleepy

Sloths are not very active. They mostly eat leaves from trees. Leaves don't give sloths much energy. Sloths save energy by moving slowly.

Sloths spend most of their lives hanging upside-down in trees.

9

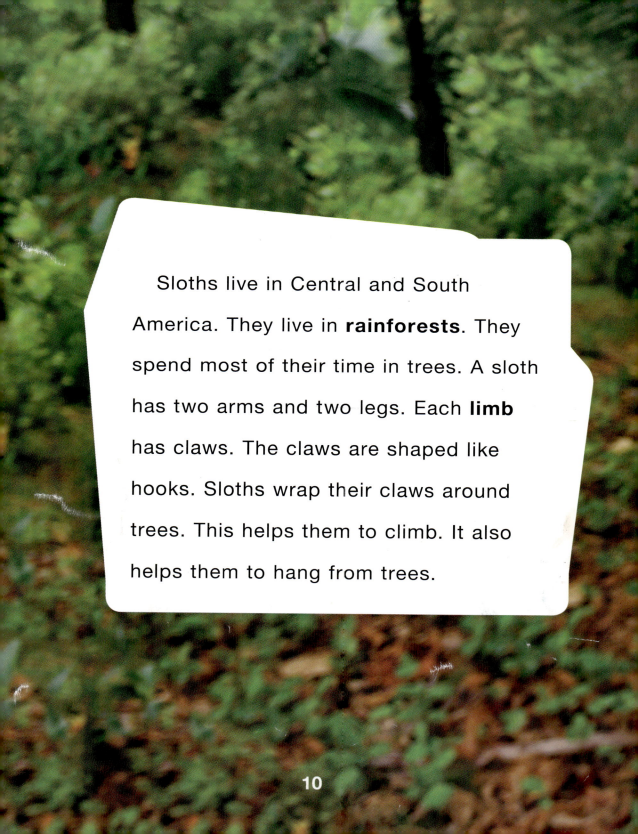

Sloths live in Central and South America. They live in **rainforests**. They spend most of their time in trees. A sloth has two arms and two legs. Each **limb** has claws. The claws are shaped like hooks. Sloths wrap their claws around trees. This helps them to climb. It also helps them to hang from trees.

Claws help sloths climb trees.

DIET AND DIGESTION

Sloths eat leaves and twigs. They get water from the leaves they eat. First, a sloth bites off a leaf. It uses its two front teeth. A sloth's lips are tough. They shred leaves up. The sloth moves its jaw. Its teeth grind the leaves.

TYPES OF SLOTHS

Sloths have three claws on each foot. Some sloths also have three claws on each hand. They are called three-toed sloths. Other sloths have two claws on each hand. They are called two-toed sloths.

Sloths smack their lips together to tear up their food.

13

Sloths can find all of the food they need in trees.

Three-toed sloths only eat leaves. But two-toed sloths also eat other foods. They sometimes eat eggs from birds' nests. They also eat insects and lizards. Some trees have flowers or fruits. Two-toed sloths eat these foods as well.

Food moves to the sloth's stomach. Then it is broken down. Leaves are hard to **digest**. The food breaks down slowly. A sloth has a large stomach. It can fit a lot of food. Digested food goes to the **intestine**. It comes out as poo.

Humans poo about 12 hours after eating. Sloths usually poo once a week.

A sloth loses weight after pooing. Its stomach shrinks. A sloth may lose up to one-third of its body weight.

Adult three-toed sloths usually weigh about 4 kilograms (9 pounds).

CHAPTER 3

SLOTH
Survival

Poo breaks are dangerous for sloths. They can be attacked by **predators**. Jaguars try to eat them. Eagles swoop down. They try to grab sloths.

Sloths stop moving when predators are near. Then predators may not notice them. Some sloths can fight if they need to. Two-toed sloths have big teeth. They fight with their claws and teeth.

The colour of a sloth's fur helps it blend in with trees to hide from predators.

A young sloth uses its claws to cling to its mother's fur.

GREEN FUR

Sloth fur is **tinted** green. This colour comes from **algae**. Algae grow on a sloth's fur. Green fur helps sloths blend into trees.

SCENT MESSAGES

Scientists aren't sure why sloths poo on the ground. Some scientists think they do this to find **mates**. Female sloths poo and wee near a tree. The wee and poo has a scent. The scent sends a message. It tells male sloths a female is in the tree.

Sloths mate in the treetops. A female hangs upside-down to give birth. The baby clings to its mother for six to nine months.

Sloths are **mammals**. All mammals make milk. A baby sloth drinks its mother's milk. The baby eats **solid** food after a few days. It poos when its mother poos.

Sloths usually have one baby at a time.

CHAPTER 4

STRONG Swimmers

Sloths sometimes need to find new trees. They may eat almost all of the food on a tree. Then they need to find more food.

Many tree leaves in rainforests have **toxins**. A toxin is a type of poison. Each tree may have a different toxin. Sloths eat from many trees. This may be so they don't get too much of one toxin.

Sloths don't usually travel more than 38 metres (125 feet) per day.

Sloths can swim almost three times faster than they can walk.

Sloths can swim. They sometimes swim across rivers or streams. They do this to get to new trees.

A sloth drops out of a tree. It lands in the water. Its limbs push it through the water.

Sloths are not speedy. They often face danger. But they are clever. They know how to survive.

GLOSSARY

algae
like a simple plant

digest
to break down food so the body can use it

intestine
an organ below the stomach that helps to digest food

limb
a part of the body that sticks out, such as an arm or a leg

mammal
a warm-blooded animal that feeds milk to its young

mate
a partner that an animal makes babies with

predator
an animal that kills and eats other animals

rainforest
a wooded area that receives a lot of rain

solid
describes something that isn't a liquid and that holds its shape

tinted
lightly coloured or dyed

toxin
a poison produced by a living thing, such as a plant

TOP FIVE REASONS WHY SLOTHS ARE AWESOME

1. They are surprisingly strong swimmers.

2. Their coats have a greenish tint due to algae growing on their fur.

3. Female sloths scream when searching for a mate. This helps male sloths find them.

4. A sloth's powerful claws continue to grip trees even after it dies.

5. Female sloths give birth while hanging upside-down from a tree branch.

ACTIVITY

Sloth digestion takes much longer than human digestion! To explore why, try this simple experiment:

WHAT YOU'LL NEED

1 slice of bread

1 bowl

¼ cup water

¼ cup vinegar

1 towel

3–4 tree leaves

INSTRUCTIONS

1. Tear up the bread into small pieces. Put the bread pieces in the bowl.

2. Pour the water and vinegar into the bowl. This liquid is like your stomach acid. It breaks down the bread.

3. Squeeze the bread with your hands. This is similar to how your stomach squeezes your food.

4. Form the bread into a ball. Take it out of the bowl. Then move it to the towel. Squeeze the liquid out of the bread ball. This is similar to how your intestine absorbs extra liquid from food. The bread ball is now like a long piece of poo!

5. Try doing this same process with the leaves. Does it work? What does this tell you about how food is digested in a sloth's stomach?

FIND OUT MORE

Ready to discover more fun facts about sloths?
Learn more with these resources.

Books

Sloths (Amazing Animals), Valerie Bodden (Creative Paperbacks, 2018)

Sloths (Nature's Children), Josh Gregory (Scholastic, 2015)

Swing Sloth! Explore the Rain Forest, Susan Newman (National Geographic Kids, 2014)

Websites

National Geographic: Sloth
kids.nationalgeographic.com/animals/sloth/#sloth-beach-upside-down.jpg

San Diego Zoo: Two-Toed Sloth
animals.sandiegozoo.org/animals/two-toed-sloth

INDEX